It Happens
to Strong
People, Too

It Happens to Strong People, Too

POEMS

Kaci Kai

Aspen and Sonder · Austin, Texas

Published by Aspen and Sonder, LLC
aspenandsonder.com

First Edition
ISBN-13: 978-1-7320614-1-5

Cover art by Fancy Tom (fancytom.com)
Book design by Kaci Kai

Table of Contents

"Go back and take care of yourself. Your body needs you, your feelings need you, your perceptions need you. Your suffering needs you to acknowledge it. Go home and be there for all these things."

—Thich Nhat Hanh

PART ONE

It All Starts Somewhere, Right?

Born on a Thursday

What happened? she asked.
I'm really good at self-sabotage, I told her.
Start from the beginning, she said.
I was born on a Thursday, I began.

On the Roof

When I was a kid
I'd climb the black wrought iron gate
That intersected the back of my house
Careful to step over the sharp points
And clamber up on the roof.

At the highest point, I'd sit
And watch clouds overhead
Watch the world below me
Cars passing on the street
A boy I liked walking by.

I thought about yelling down
To show him I wasn't afraid
But I watched silently instead
He never saw me.

People are something to fear
I guess that's the takeaway here
I'll climb the tallest building
And try just about anything once
But to call out
And say
Look! Look at me!
That invites a verdict
It's safer to sit alone
And watch it all pass below.

Trains

At night, the train barrels past
And if I'm lucky I'll catch it just as I slip into sleep.
It's one of the few sounds I remember
Of the house I grew up in.

I heard it every day for the first 15 years of my life.
And it offered a steady heartbeat
To an otherwise terrorizing quiet.

Movement and possibility—
I fantasized about jumping on one day—
In the place of a perfect stagnant pond
Where mosquitoes thrived.

Now when I roll into sleep
With that sound in my head
I think fondly of a place
That I couldn't wait to escape.

Scars and Dirt

Can you pick at scars
Until they become
Flesh wounds again?

Or do you pick
Until scar tissue opens up
To something new?

Forced to repeat
Until lessons finally learned
Rolling back and forth
Over the same goddamn red dirt
A reminder that you came from land
That stains your clothes
And if anyone gets too close
It'll stain their clothes too.

Like a Footnote

When she was asked to tell her story
She gave it three lines
Before stepping back
And asking someone else
And you?

An internal sigh
Relief
This is much more interesting.

She told her life like a footnote.

I Miss the Sun

The darkness protected her
From being seen
A shield
So they couldn't make out her stripes.

They'll love me
As long as they don't see me too clearly.

And they did.

She was always a bit blurry around the edges
But at least they loved her.

I miss the sun, she thought,
As the horizon started to turn
As she went inside.

Luminescence

I look best in the dark
Silhouetted to an outline
The whites of my eyes
Almonds against the night.

From this place
I can see the magic in me
Luminescent and cool
A pale blue
Just barely visible.

Maybe it's why I'm reserved
Purposefully set in darkness
Trying to find that place
Where I emit light
Without stirring up a fire.

Trying not to be seen
Sliding along the edge
So I can watch others
In their incandescence.

A House for Commitment

She built her house
In the tallest tree she could find
With no ladder up to her front door.
There, she thought.
Now only the most committed will visit.

PART TWO

Gains and Losses

Instead

When he arrived
I announced I was gay
Like a surname.

But then he spoke poetry to me
In forms I'd never heard before
It didn't matter
What names I called myself
He was patient
And never cast judgment.

It was in a stairwell
Knees pressed to my chin
Hands grasping my shins
Between
My skater shoes
And skater shorts
Long blonde hair, dirty red at the ends
He asked me to say more
That I decided, soundless,
I was a bisexual instead.

It Tastes Like This,
Because It Is This

Do you taste the fruity tartness?
Maybe something in the Honeycrisp family
Zippy
Yet
Dipped in honey
Yet
Crunchy
Hands meeting as we pick up another slice.

I taste more of the earthy notes
Kind of like coffee on a rainy January day
Our feet touching under thick blankets.

It sort of tastes like when the tomatoes come in
Early Girl if you're lucky
Picked right from the vine
I hold them in my hand
And feed them to you
Still warm.

It tastes a little like Texas peaches
Sticky sweetness, into a pie
Homemade crust and all
I give you the best piece I can cut
Smiling at you as I lick my fingers.
It tastes like love, doesn't it?

We Were Rich: A Snack Dinner

Tonight for dinner
I collect Varzi, a coarse ground salami
From a town in Italy by the same name.

Green Castelvetrano olives
Buttery, salty richness.

My favorite 5-year aged Gouda
Smoky, dry perfection.

Paté and coarse mustard piled
On slivers of toasted baguette.
Your favorite.

A bottle of Barolo
Rich, dry, and drinkable.

And for dessert,
Burrata
With basil and peaches.

We were rich.
It was poetry,
A love note to each other.

Pay Up

I've been spending goodness
And accumulating debt from it.
Like it's not really anything I ever possessed.
I was just borrowing it. On loan.
It's time to pay up.

The Day It Went Sideways

The first day
I started to go sideways
I seem to remember
I was walking down the sidewalk
Thinking about the cracks
In the concrete
Spiderwebbing out in front of me
And then somehow
Mid-thought
It all started to turn
A solid 90 degrees
I've been walking on edges of buildings
Along tree trunks
Across parked car doors
And people's faces
Jumping over windows and exit signs
Ever since

What Is There to Say?

There was a moment in our movie
When I should have said
Stay. Stay. *We'll figure it out together.*
But I have cotton in my mouth.
I'm numb and mute.

I watched you fall asleep and
I thought it would be easier
If this really was a brain tumor
Pushing on some part of my personality
Pushing on me to do the unthinkable.
I wonder if anyone has ever died from crying.
I think about heart attacks.
My heart hurts in my chest.
Not figuratively. My heart hurts.

I lie in your arms,
I don't know what to say.
I'm a futurist and a planner.
Tomorrow you become my past.
What is there to say when tomorrow is goodbye?

Disordered

The heat clamped down on my appetite,
suppressing all interest in food. Every time I'd
lift my fork to my mouth, a queasy, wrenching
would start in my stomach and travel up
my esophagus.

I ate two meals a day over many hours. One tiny,
nauseating bite at a time. Light meals of lettuce
and cucumbers and tomatoes and eggs. My
caloric intake was probably half what I needed.

On the third day, I woke up sick in my own skin.
Hip bones jutting. Hard edges, creaky and
exposed, a thin layer of skin. All skeleton.

I became dizzy walking to the bathroom, my
vision filling with the pins and needles static
from early black-and-white televisions and I
gripped the edge of the sink to keep from
spilling over.

It took me an hour to make a simple meal: two
eggs fried in olive oil, chorizo, raw tomatoes,
lettuce, and cilantro folded in two flour tortillas,
a side of raw yellow bell peppers and cucumbers,
a cup of coffee.

And another two hours to eat it.

Mettle

A colleague riffed
And the words "testing your mettle" came out.
I had to keep my face straight
Because in that moment
I knew I'd failed you.
My metal was tested
And it crumbled
On the battlefield
Where my demons fought.
Maybe I was water the whole time.
Or maybe air and wood and fire
Supplying and building
A fantastic version of our collective hell.

Things That Make Me Sad*

Weddings
Brides and grooms taking pictures in public
Exceptionally delicious meals
Children
Couples in love
Couples showing affection
Traveling
Technology
Phone maintenance
Stars
Space
Science
Family photos
Big cooking events
Frank Sinatra
Lamb
Roast potatoes
Rosemary
January
April
Thanksgiving
Christmas
New Years
Halloween
Pictures of you
The smell of fresh lavender
The blue grey color that was our living room
When someone mispronounces the silent E in our
last name
Saturday mornings: breakfast, coffee, cartoons

That song—"Lovin' You"
Fall
Decent bath towels

*** *** ***

*And by sad,
I mean
Suicidal. But I promised.
Sadness so deep,
They're gashes cut through me.
A pain,
A missing heart and lung and arm and spleen.

And by sad,
I mean it's like sucking in air
Like water through a straw and still
Expecting to breathe.

And by sad,
I mean my face is no longer a mask.

And by sad,
I mean I'm sorry.

How to Cry

The need to cry
Feels like the need to vomit
Standing in the shower
Willing myself
In the same way
I'd curl my body
Over a toilet bowl
Praying to evacuate my stomach.

I woke up this morning with ghosts
In my head.
Full.
I feel hungover.

And I still can't figure out how to cry.

Vacillation

I've been vacillating
Between severely open
Cut wide
And closed
Tight tight tight.
I'm on a pendulum and
Neither feels very good right now.
It's making me reclusive, lazy.
The grey days aren't helping.

Keep It Together

Today I'm trying to keep it together.
I'm a pot simmering
Two seconds from boiling over.
If I stare too hard
Or think too much
I'm going to lose control.
And I'll cry until
The pot dries out.
I'll cry so long and so hard
I might start a fire
And burn this city to the ground.

Foreign Foods

You send me a list of food
But the words—even in my native tongue
—seem foreign.

It's been so long
Since I've thought of food like this.
Our love notes.

I stare at the words
And I squint and click my tongue
Against the roof of my mouth
Three little ticks
Trying to snatch a taste of it from the air.

You are over a thousand miles away
Those dishes are nothing but words on the page.
I'm numb to anything resembling love.

But I'm starving.

Closing Your Eyes

Closing my eyes feels so good
I wonder if this is what it feels like when you die
When the feeling of closing your eyes
Outweighs the feeling of keeping them open

I Lost Weight

I lost a bunch of weight
While trying to find myself in paradise.

Four months of hard-earned muscle
Eaten away in a month
By depression and heat and remorse.

My clothes hang on me now
And I wonder if I'll know I'm whole again
When I fit into my jeans
Like I did before.

The Memory

The memory I'd pay the most to erase...
I flick through the internal photo album
Of bad memories
But not one crystallizes into a definite answer.

Maybe it'd be the look on your face
As we sat on the cool white tiles of our kitchen
Crying.
Or the way you looked
As you left our apartment in Montreal.
Or the way your face twisted
An expression
I'd never seen before
As I destroyed what we'd built.

But I don't think it's fair
To discard these memories
Because the biggest price I could ever pay
Is to remember them.

It Was a Miracle

For long moments
I think about the process of healing.

I close my eyes
Lift my head
And try to will myself
To heal.

And in that moment she was healed.
Lo! It was a miracle, they'd say.
Their hands raised to the sky in exultation.

Please, I whisper into the stillness.
Please, I don't want to feel this anymore.

And when the roar of the waves
Comes barreling up
Out of my diaphragm
From depths deeper than the deepest below
A storm of emotions
You could have seen coming for days
Rumbles out.
My throat raw and hoarse now.

I beg to not feel it.

Please, I cry out into the hurricane.
Please, I don't want to feel this anymore.

And in that moment, she was numb.
Lo, it was a miracle.
She was numb.

Where Bombs Were Dropped

Staring at my palm
Tracing the lines
In my hand
Looking for a clue
To my future
I wonder if
I could have predicted
This moment.
I trace the lines again
Looking for a bump
Or an indication
But the lines in my hand
Look like a war zone
Hash marks written
In my skin
Like grooves
In the dirt
Where bombs
Were dropped.

Help Where I Can Get It

Maybe it's time I admit to you
I'm terrified of emotions.
Terror is an emotion, right?
Yeah, I'm extra cozy with fear.

Right now, I'd volunteer
To jump out of airplanes
To get into the ring
To leap off a bridge
To drive fast
To travel someplace alone

But heaven help me
If I see a mildly sad commercial
About thin toilet paper.

Zeus grant me the strength
To weather the effects
Of a birth announcement.

Allah afford me the power to survive
A sweet couple's 50th wedding anniversary.

Christ provide me resiliency against
The absurd injustices of the world.
The Trumps.
The oil spills.
The masses of floating plastic.

Great Goddess protect me from the pain
Of hearing songs of deep emotion.

I'm afraid to ask for help.
I'm afraid to feel the love that grows.
I'm afraid to meet your gaze.
To be seen or heard.
Or to feel anything at all.

I started to feel some variation of happiness
The other day
And in a panic I reminded myself
Audibly
This was dangerous territory
Shut it down.

Honey and Charcoal

It's honey and charcoal
I suck at them both
Covering my fingers

I've convinced people
It's delicious.
And sometimes it is.

She smiles at me and tilts her head
Not understanding what I've just said

I lift my fingers for her to inspect
And she blinks to understand

My gaze flits between her face
Stunned and silent
And my hand
Obvious as can be

It's just honey and charcoal.

A Tiny Truth

And this is where I tell you a tiny,
Unnamed, vague truth
Because I'm too much of a coward to tell
you openly.

I was in the business of beating myself up.

I asked for Punishment
And he found me.
He did his work.

Until it was time to leave and
A new choice was made.

I'm very lucky
Punishment released me
And I had good people
On the other side
To catch what was left.

Where It Hurts

And here?
He asks
Pointing to the bruise
Size of a lime
On my left bicep.

I shake my head.
No, not there.

And what about here?
He points to my elbow
Rubbed raw
I'm shaking my head again.
He points to the other elbow
Same story?

Not there, I repeat.

And here?
He pushes the paper up
To expose more of the purple and blue
That takes up most of my left thigh.

I rub my fingers over the edges
That space between pale pink skin
And the thunderstorm
Rolling in.

No, I say.

He lifts his eyebrows at that one.

Down at my left foot
The spot just below my big toe is swollen.

This looks like it hurts, he says examining it closer.
He presses at the space around the swelling.

I'm quiet now.
He looks up.

It's here then, he says.

No.

Where? He asks.
If not here, then where?

It hurts. Right here.
Pointing at the clearest, softest area
Protected by my ribs.
The part no one ever thinks to check.
In the middle, I say.

It Happens to Strong People, Too

It's happened to a lot of strong people, he said.
It's not something to be ashamed of.
I smiled. Sad.
I'd given up my power.

But that usually happens earlier
And then they go get strong,
Not the other way around.

Not always, he said.

Bones and Mistakes

I wonder what stories we tell ourselves
How we hold on to the people we once were
So we don't lose sight of ourselves
Growing into something different and foreign.

Human beings are not static creatures.
We flow and bend and mold into the next phase
Like wax melting onto a table.
You'd think it was destruction,
But really it's a new sculpture I made
From my bones and my mistakes.
A new map spread out
In blood red across the dark wood grain
My fingerprints pressed
A sign that
Some version of myself
Was here.

PART THREE

The Turn

Inhale. And, Nothing.

Inhale.
And, nothing.
There's supposed to be something after that
My breath is caught
Suspended
What comes after inhale?
I try not to panic
But I can feel my heart pound
Maybe it's... more inhale?
I suck in a little more breath
And feel my lungs almost explode
I close my eyes
It was supposed to be so easy
Just one foot in front of the other
So I take a step
But that's not it either
Where to go from here?
What comes next I wonder
As my lips turn blue
My eyes bulging
Inhale.
And, then...

A Letter I Never Sent
(And Should Have)

Dear friends, family, colleagues,
and acquaintances,

I regret to inform you I broke his heart.
I broke mine too. He's not the bad guy you want
him to be on my behalf. There's no need for
congratulations. Not even a need for condolences.

Sometimes people implode. Make mistakes.
Make choices. Sometimes you need something
to end. Sometimes you wish it hadn't even if it's
what you needed at the time. And sometimes,
people are masters in self-sabotage.

But—*dear people in my life*—I am a carefully
crafted human being trying to hide my life's
traumas. I never wanted you to see this side of
me. As if I ever had a choice in the matter.
Sometimes those come raging out in a fantastic
show of fireworks. Sometimes there's no
recovering from that.

The pessimist in me would tell you all good
things end. The nihilist would tell you I'm so
insignificant it doesn't matter anyway.
The heartbroken would tell you I hope I never
feel again. The optimist says something beautiful
will come from this.

What I need from you, here on out, is to know
I don't need you to cast shadows. Be a beacon.

Many thanks and much love,
Kac

Try Not to Fall

The more I push against
The more it pulls me in
No choice
But to go with the flow
Or give in eventually
To the exhaustion.

There comes a time
When you have to trust
This ocean, this life
You have to respect it
Feel it pull you and then push you back
And know it's taking you to the right place
For you.
Just keep your head above water
Keep breathing
And rolling with it all.

Try not to flail
As the push becomes a pull
Try not to fail
As the pull becomes a push again.
Try not to fall.

Cycles

The full moon sets over the Pacific
In a pastel pink haze
Just as the sun rises
Casting brilliance into shadow.

What a world we live in
To see a reflection
In front of us
Of that which creeps up behind.

If you wait long enough
This cyclical affair
Will happen again.
What will you do differently next time?

In This Place, at This Time

A year seems so long ago
How much things have changed
And yet I'm still basically me
Coming out into another place.

I emerge from the dark forest
Eyes squinting, mouth dry with eternal thirst
Asking the nearest passerby what day it is
Okay, what *year*.
Gasping at all the time that's passed.

There's a lot of judgment
In how someone spends their time.
I chose every step
And still there are days I wake up
Amazed that I'm here
In this place, at this time.

I love looking at cause and effect
Inspecting the choices we make
And how they lead us to where we are.

In movies I predict how it will turn in the end
And I'm always disappointed when I'm right.
When we take a little trip someplace unexpected
I'm delighted, fascinated.
How? I think.
How did the plot twist to this place, at this time?

I Choose

And then there are days
When I make big decisions
Things I've been considering
Between two places.
And then
That's it
The choice is made.
I've suffered enough.
No one was ever keeping score anyway.
Self-flagellation is not atonement.

I'm leaving. No.
I'm changing.
I'm staying.
I'm healing.
I'm teaching.

I choose to decide
Therefore I do.

I choose to be connected
Therefore I am.

I choose to be better.

The Perfect Fruit Tray

I inspect every option
As if the perfect fruit tray
Will make them like me more.

I scrutinize the fruit
The strawberries
Red and perfect on the outside
I pray they're not rotten inside
As they so often are.

The melons are bruised on the outside
Visible scars across their mottled skin
But I know from experience
That this can make for the sweetest flavor.

The peaches are soft
Too soft
At the press of my thumb
It could be damage
Or this one could just be extra juicy.

I study every option
As if this decision will distract
From the reality of who I am
But I've promised myself now
To be unapologetically me
Whatever the consequences.

Do you like apples? Watermelon? Pineapple?
Just... Please like me.

Lint

We go around the circle
And dump out our pockets
Everyone has something
They were protecting
Down beneath even the lint.

Skeletons

I guess when you realize
It's not just you
Everyone has a skeleton inside
It's easier to see
What's inside of me
Is also inside of you.

Stay Weird

It's easy to say
Stay you
Stay weird
Your tribe is out there
And they'll love you
It's easy to say those words
But to live them
Is something else
Altogether

Two Lionesses

We lounged on her L-shaped white couch
And she told me about her Lion Tribe.
How long it had taken her to realize
She'd been trying too hard to fit in with the gazelles
But she's no gazelle.

Nothing wrong with them, she said.
They're just a different species and I'm a lion.
You're part of the tribe, she told me.

My shock obvious.
She smiled and waited.

But I think I'm a gazelle, I said,
My voice small. A child's.
And she looked at me
Almost pitying.

It took me a moment
Longer than it should have.

I'm a lion too, aren't I?
She smiled a toothy grin.

But look at my little gazelle ears, I joked,
Pretending to shift them on my head.

Two blonde lionesses lounging on the sofa
Hands draped like paws over the edge.

We laughed and laughed.

The Art Is Crooked

The art on the wall
Is crooked.

A mosaic
A collage of found objects
Shells and tiles
Blue square waves
Rolling in a square world.
A famous quote
About smooth seas and skilled sailors.

The piece is crooked
Which is funny to me
I get the joke.
I don't fix it.

Days Between the Darkness

Leaving the gym at 2 p.m. on a Wednesday
Music blaring
Windows down
Sweat drying on my skin
A memory from the night before
I tap my fingers on the steering wheel
And take a right on South First.

This feeling I have
This fleeting, generous moment
Is it real?
Or is this just me
Taking a breath between
The shit I felt yesterday
And the shit I'll feel tomorrow?

Or is this the very definition of life
Trying to accumulate more days like this
—The sun warm on my skin,
Endorphins high,
A kiss on my lips—
Between the darkness?

The Best Sunsets

You would think a clear evening
Would produce the best sunsets
But I propose the sunsets
That leave me sitting and staring
Long after they're gone
In awe
Are the skies with cellulite
Wrinkles and folds
Shit has gone down in those currents somewhere
And now look at the purples and golds
A series of events that forged this landscape
Even more beautiful than the day before.

The Stories We Tell Ourselves

We like to talk about new beginnings
But it's disingenuous to ignore
Everything that happened before.

This is no beginning
And it's no end either.

Because the beginning happened
When your parents decided to give you life.

No, even before then,
Your beginning happened
When your grandparents decided
To give your parents li...
No, even before.

See the trouble with beginnings?
Our stories started before us
Turned and shaped
By a host of other narratives
Long before your physical form.

And the end?
You think it's when you die?
What about the waves you sent sweeping
The ripples from the stones you
Dropped, or placed, or threw?

That's what I realized
When I decided it was time to stop hurting
I'm not in the end
Or the beginning

I'm still somewhere in the middle
And that means I can change what happens next.

Right here
I can change everything

If I just choose a better story.

Endeavor

I am happy
I am healthy
I am safe
I am strong
I am worthy
I am whole
I am good

THE END

If you enjoyed this...

Sign up for Kaci Kai's email newsletter to receive notifications of future releases, free poems, discounts, and more at kacikai.com/newsletter.

Become a patron at patreon.com/kacikai.

Please also take a few minutes to write a review of *It Happens to Strong People, Too* on amazon.com and goodreads.com. Thanks!

Finally, sign up for Aspen and Sonder's newsletter for future project announcements at aspenandsonder.com/newsletter

Collaborations

I petitioned my friends for poem prompts. These poems in particular allowed me to write parts of this story I hadn't been able to articulate yet. For each of these collaborators, I thank you for seeing me and for participating in my poetry. Thank you.

I Miss The Sun
Ranna Bigdely

It Tastes Like This, Because It Is This
Zeke Leonard

The Memory
Elizabeth Beal

Where It Hurts
Amy Winters

Inhale. And, Nothing.
Eva Agaeva

Try Not to Fall
Allison Burch

The Best Sunsets
Julie Campbell

Acknowledgments

Thank you, first and foremost, to my sister, Kerry Higdon. Thank you for your guidance, your time, your careful and precise eye, your sharp memory, your kind words and encouragement, and your unwavering belief in me. The best decision our parents ever made was having you.

Jeff Isacksen, thank you for being you: kind, compassionate, brilliant, giving, and hilarious. Thank you for being there when I needed you most, through the tricky parts of living. I'm so lucky.

Amy Winters, thank you for giving me your precious and limited time to read what I created and giving me exactly what I needed. And thank you for cultivating the place I call home. I owe you. We owe you.

Allison Burch, thank you for your time, care, kindness, humor, and your brilliant editor eye. You always give the best advice—in life and in writing. Thank you.

Fancy Tom, so many thanks for sharing your art with me. You continue to be an inspiration. We've got work to do. Extra special thanks for giving me permission to use your painting as my cover art.

—

Thank you to Elizabeth Beal for sharing your poetry and your life with me. Your words have always reached down deep. I aspire to write even in the same ballpark as you.

Thank you, Jolyn Janis, for reaching out, sharing your work and your world, and for giving me tough love. You are light and beauty and strength.

Thank you to my mom for instilling in me a stubborn belief that I can do anything. Just try and tell me I can't. Just try.

Thank you to my dad for encouraging me more than once to write and publish a book. You've always encouraged my creativity—from my first SLR and beyond. Thank you.

Thank you, also, to my Patreon patrons. In particular, I'd like to thank Alex the Ward. Holy crap, thank you.

Finally, thank you, CL. *Thank you.*

About the Author

Kaci Kai's childhood nickname was Crazy Kaci.

She once fought a girl in a ring in Thailand. And won. She sold all her possessions and traveled as a nomad for more than a year. She jumped out of an airplane. Twice (and counting). Swam with sharks. Bungee jumped. She won two cooking competitions. And chased tornadoes with her dad as a kid. She prefers the brutal, dry heat of Texas summers to anything below 70° F.

But the scariest, craziest thing she's done to date? She wrote and published *It Happens to Strong People, Too.*

Kaci Kai is a writer and publisher living in Austin, Texas.

kacikai.com

About the Publisher

Aspen and Sonder is a small media/publishing company in Austin, Texas.

We share complicated human stories, especially stories that tell a central truth—in real life there is no good or evil. There are only the stories we tell ourselves.

Sign up for their newsletter to hear about future releases.

aspenandsonder.com

About the Type

It Happens to Strong People, Too was set in Libre Baskerville, a typeface designed by Pablo Impallari.

Baskerville was originally designed by John Baskerville (1706–1775) in the 1750s in Birmingham, England and cut into metal by punchcutter John Handy.

Libre Baskerville is an updated typeface based on the American Type Founder's 1941 version of Baskerville. It features a taller x-height, wider counters, and less contrast than it's predecessors.

10264211R00047

Made in the USA
San Bernardino, CA
28 November 2018